RISK, RECOVERY, AND EMPOWERMENT

THE KAZAKHSTAN BANK RESTRUCTURE CASE STUDY

MARCIA-ELIZABETH C. FAVALE

ISBN (paperback) 979-8-9861308-0-4

eBook ISBN 979-8-9861308-1-1

PRAISE

"The bankruptcy petition filed in the United States Bankruptcy Court for the Southern District of New York by Lehman Brothers on September 15, 2008, set off a world-wide economic nightmare. Its shock waves threatened a global depression. Marcia Elizabeth C. Favale's book, Risk, Recovery, and Empowerment: The Kazakhstan Bank Restructure Case Study walks the reader through how she constructed a "Burden-Sharing" restructuring strategy for three of Kazakhstan's biggest banks that were teetering on failure in the wake of Lehman's bankruptcy. Her strategy brought together conflicting interests of key stakeholders (bank management, depositors, shareholders, creditors, and government entities), which resulted in a hard-fought success for these divergent stakeholders and the people of Kazakhstan. We should all learn from Ms. Favale's strategy."

—Paul Regan,
CPA, *author of* The Forensic: How the CIA, a Brilliant Attorney, and a Young CPA Brought Down Howard Hughes

"When you combine the emotional intelligence of a great leader, along with the methodologies and control systems of project management, you get the positive outcome that the people of Kazakhstan did. This is not your everyday case study. Marcia Favale's efforts culminated in a masterpiece that now, with this book, we can all bear witness to."

—Maureen Lippe,
Lippe Taylor PR & Digital Marketing,
author of *Radical Reinvention*

"A provocative read to be sure. Marcia Favale shares a practical but compelling map of economic history in a unique transcontinental country and demonstrates the power of one person's innovation, knowledge, expedient strategy, and courage to go—literally and figuratively—where the masses are not going. This is a timeless case study with important lessons for all governments. When Marcia talks, listen."

—Pete Biolsi,
SVP, Pricing and Profitability, Bank of America

"Effective strategists always have the ability to set a vision, solve problems, and rise above prosaic matters—especially when real people, real economics are at stake. What Favale accomplished is nothing short of brilliant."

—David Carlucci,
former New York State Senator (2011-2020)

"Drive business and cultural priorities 5,000 miles away from 'home'? Check. Demonstrate agility, empathetic leadership, comprehension of intricate factors and how the outcome will affect millions? Check. Risk taker and champion of a new solution rather than the safe route? That's her, too. And Marcia Favale triumphed. I would recommend this book to every project management student and guru alike for its rare, riveting insights."

—Loretta Cate, D.Ph., CPCC

"Marcia Favale managed to avoid the traps and status quo from the economic collapse that rocked the world when bailouts reigned. Her intellectual vastness shines through in Risk, Recovery, and Empowerment, but I am most taken by her fearless leadership that drove an international benchmark. Sharing this case study in 2022 is no coincidence—it's urgently needed!"

—Scott N. Zambelli,
Managing Partner, Heritage Harbor Financial Associates

The Headlines

"Kazakh banks had borrowed heavily to fund an oil-driven domestic consumer boom but were stranded with $45bn of foreign debt when the US subprime crisis erupted."

—Financial Times

"International banks will lend their expertise in areas such as valuation, due diligence and ensuring international best practice."

—Euromoney

*"Kazakhstan's BTA Bank has reached a
deal over its trade finance debt."*

—Global Trade Review

*"Between 2000 and 2011, Kazakhstan's economy grew by an
average of 8.4 per cent. The country's foreign policy has proven
effective in balancing international interests as Kazakhstan continues
to forge its path into international and regional organizations."*

—Economist Impact

"A Kazakh horror show nears its ending."

—Eurasia

*"Problems raised by the restructuring of non-sovereign entities
were dealt with in a very concrete manner, notably thanks
to the participation of Mrs. Marcia Favale-Tarter."*

—Institute of International Finance's Conference
on Sustainable Financing of Emerging and
Developing Countries

DEDICATION

I dedicate this book to my daughter, Alexandra Elizabeth.

Contents

ACKNOWLEDGMENTS

No journey is forged alone. I thank the government officials, fellow advisors, steering committee members, the press that gave fair coverage, management of the banks and especially Grigori Marchenko, governor of the National Bank, who gave me the opportunity and championed its success.

To the readers, and though we have never met, I hope this book provides inspiration. Love the word "no". Listen to how people want you to fail and take that precious insight and use it to mitigate the risk and propel you to success.

Special thanks to Candi Cross, my editor, who worked with me on this book with great enthusiasm and expertise.

FOREWORD

The Kazakhstan bank restructuring in 2009-2010 was an outstanding effort of our country to achieve a difficult but fair solution for all the parties concerned, and Marcia played a key role in that effort. I am the guy who insisted that she be hired to do the restructuring.

I was appointed for my second term as a governor of National Bank of Kazakhstan in late January 2009, to tackle two large problems at once: 1. Our large neighbor and our largest trading partner then, Russia, devalued its currency, the ruble, by 50%, and we had to do a compensatory devaluation to protect our markets. The tenge had fallen by 25% on Feb. 4, which was hugely criticized at the time, but proved to be a timely and efficient measure. And 2. We knew that at least three of our ten largest banks would be hit hard by the devaluation as they had clearly over-borrowed in the international capital markets during the boom years (2005-2007). Over 60% of BTA Bank and Temir Bank liabilities and over 70% of Alliance Bank debt was in foreign currencies. We had to either restructure their foreign debt or liquidate them in an orderly manner. The third option—bailing them out by the state using taxpayers' money (which was a heavily preferred option in the West)—was briefly discussed, but the ticket price was way too heavy for the state.

Adhering to market practice, the banks hired investment banks and law firms through a tender process to represent them in negotiations with affected investors, but we also decided to hire our own consultants who would steadfastly defend our country's interests. I suggested that Marcia be hired on the banking side and John Howell on the legal side. When investment banks are hired for such complex and controversial restructurings, they tend to listen more to the other side for obvious reasons; our side is not an important client for them, whereby on the other side of the table you have dozens of large investment funds, insurance companies, commercial banks, and Eximbanks. So, in the end, they usually are biased and tend to present a solution, which "the market requires" and which is usually unfair to a developing country and/or its banks. And it was the first of the novelties of our approach, which was hugely beneficial, as Marcia proved her worth to the deal many times over.

The Kazakhstan bank restructuring program was a lengthy, difficult, complicated, innovative and, at times, exasperating deal, but we eventually came out with flying colors, and we have to thank Marcia for that to a very large degree, though it was definitely a team effort and a lot of people were involved. When the final deal was signed, several representatives of investors came to me and thanked me for being treated fairly and it was the most important part. In a deal like that, every party must lose something, but the losses should be distributed objectively, and nobody should feel being taken advantage of.

I highly recommend this book, as it could be very useful for everyone who could be involved in any type of debt restructuring, and there are very many of us in this world.

—Grigori Marchenko,
former governor, National Bank of Kazakhstan
(1999-2004, 2009-2013)

PREFACE

*"Not many people are prepared to go to developing
countries and make change. It's not just about change.
Developing countries also influence developed countries.
Many processes are dependent on each other."*

—Marat Beketayev,
former Minister of Justice, Republic of Kazakhstan

ON MONDAY, SEPTEMBER 15, 2008, at 1:45 a.m., Lehman Brothers Holdings Inc. filed a bankruptcy petition in the United States Bankruptcy Court for the Southern District of New York. It was the largest bankruptcy proceeding in U.S. history. The 164-year-old firm was the fourth-largest U.S. investment bank, and its bankruptcy kicked off a global financial crisis. Countries, companies, and banks couldn't go to the market to refinance. Bankruptcies, liquidations, and restructurings exploded.

Over 5,000 miles away from New York, a controlled panic echoed across Astana, the capital of Kazakhstan, the largest country of Central Asia and ninth largest in the world in terms of size, as it did globally. This amazing country blends ancient elements and modern amenities. I can attest to this because Kazakhstan's like a second home to me.

My journey with Kazakhstan started in 2002 when I landed with our UBS capital markets team. I was the head of CEMEA and LATAM corporate bond research out of UBS London. I continued to be professionally tied to Kazakhstan throughout my investment banking and hedge fund career. However, it was in 2009, in the dead of the winter, during the financial crisis that I embarked on a career-defining mission: Restructure three banks simultaneously, whilst creating an international benchmark. This journey started with the governor of the National Bank, Grigori Marchenko, having the courage to invite me to think outside the box.

International capital markets were practically closed, causing a liquidity crunch. Emerging markets were being battered and currencies hammered. Kazakhstan was not immune. Deteriorating asset quality and the devaluation of the Kazakhstan currency, Tenge (KZT), pressured banks' balance sheets. At the height of the crisis, BTA Bank, Alliance Bank and Temir Bank needed recapitalization. Their balance sheets reflected the effects of closed capital markets, the economic slowdown, and poor risk management. BTA Bank, one of the largest in assets, was of particular concern given the impact that a disorderly collapse would have on the payment and banking system. Kazakhstan was considered in investment cycles to be one of the best banking systems in the region.

After being briefed for about twenty-four hours by the banking authorities and bank management at the offices of the chairman of Samruk-Kazyna, I understood that the stakes were high. Knock-on effects of a BTA Bank collapse were enormous. There were two other banks in trouble (Alliance Bank and Temir Bank), and allegations of fraud underpinned the poor asset qualities. I had to figure out if the government of Kazakhstan should adopt the sovereign bailout approach implemented by the developed economies for systemic banks or if an innovative alternative approach could be implemented. Global investment bankers were pressing government to bail-out investors.

On February 10, 2009, as I walked into the frigid wind of the steps towards the prime minister's office, I drew a deep breath and said to myself, *the best approach is to create a new one*. And we did. The Burden-Sharing Framework was born, and an international benchmark was made. That month, I became the senior advisor to the prime minister of Kazakhstan, Karim Massimov.

bailout—a general term for extending financial support to a company or a country facing a potential bankruptcy threat. It can take the form of loans, cash, bonds, or stock purchases. A bailout may or may not require reimbursement and is often accompanied by greater government oversee and regulations. The reason for bailout is to support an industry that may be affecting millions of people internationally and could be on the verge of bankruptcy due to prolonged financial crises. (The Economic Times)

The Burden-Sharing Framework/restructuring strategy—*has four pillars as its foundation: liquidity support, preservation of the sovereign's fiscal profile, curtailment of moral hazard, and improvements in corporate governance. The plan envisioned creditor participation through steering committees that negotiated amongst themselves by creating inter-equity dynamic tension. Restructuring strategies enveloped asset recovery as part of the value-proposition for creditors.*

INTRODUCTION

INNOVATING FISCAL RESPONSIBILITY

"I give the government carte blanche to take any steps for stabilization of economy and financial system and large powers for making any unconventional decisions required under the conditions. The government and the National Fund will be personally responsible for the stability of the economy, financial system, and social projects."

—President Nazarbayev,
New Europe Online, October 20, 2008

THE KAZAKHSTAN BURDEN-SHARING Restructuring Program is considered an international benchmark when bank restructuring programs are discussed and analyzed amongst policymakers and experts[1]. It is also the subject matter of a University of Oxford[2] case study taught at Said Business School and the Blavat-

---

1 The author presented on the restructuring program at the Paris Club meetings in 2010 and contributed an article to the 2010 Paris Club Annual Report titled "Breaking the Mold."

2 Banking Sector Restructuring Program in Kazakhstan-BTA Bank JSC by Atif Ansar and Ariell Ahearn, 25 May 2015

nik School of Government, where it was first presented. The case study is dynamic, given that the Restructuring Program adopted by Kazakhstan was innovative in its strategy and in its implementation process by advocating a bail-in strategy as opposed to the creditor-preferred bail-out.

The Kazakhstan Restructuring Program rejected the notions that a government must bail-out investors and that austerity is the 'necessary evil' for a path of fiscal stability, placing citizens ahead of investors. As notably, the Kazakhstan Restructuring Program debunked the notion that countries need to bow to the exigencies of inherently conflicted intermediaries by having its $23.4 billion restructuring program (first round of restructuring) led by an independent restructuring advisor, placing the center of power at government, not international financial centers.

From Risk to Empowerment

This book is a qualitative, investigative, and critical analysis of the post-completion phase of the $23.4 billion Burden-Sharing Kazakhstan Restructuring program (Restructuring Program). The book aims to encourage policymakers and practitioners to evaluate the legacy effects major financial restructuring programs can have on a country and to devise and design programs considering these effects upon the economy and the people. Given that major financial programs can substantially impact not only the population of a country, stakeholders, and policymakers but also, other economies and vested interests, due to the globalized structure of economic growth and funding, major financial programs are an important area for further academic studies within the major program management discourse.

The analytical framework of *Risk, Reconstruction, and Empowerment* is to answer to what extent did the Restructuring Program create legacy effects. Imbedded in the question is the notion that the Restructuring Program was a "major program." Analytical content is therefore, drawn from major program academic literature, which is not unified in its definition of *legacy*, as the concept is arguably vague (Gold and Gold: 2008), or *legacy effects*, although there are common themes. For the purposes of this book, legacy is defined to "…cover many different aspects including *image, economics, built environment and sustainability*" (Davis, and Thornely: 2010; p. 89) because these have longevity and lingering impact.

This book discusses the following:

- The context under which Kazakhstan was operating, including concerns and demands imposed by the financial crisis.

- Government's management of the crisis and therefore, the objectives in implementing the innovative Burden-Sharing Restructuring Framework.

- Legacy effects, by unbundling definitions present in academic literature, reducing the same to the core themes in order to compare certain legacy effects within the Kazakhstan context. These core legacy themes include the political dimension (Hall and Hodges; 1996)[3], macroeconomic impact (Kasimati and Dawson: 2009), sustainability, image and built environment (Davis and Thornely: 2010). The analysis excludes, as irrelevant for this analysis, other aspects such as urban regeneration (Davis and Thornley 2010) and excluded groups (Minnaert; 2001), which are not contextually meaningful.

---

3 See Hall & Hodges (1996). The research highlight that often focus on legacy is on the economic dimension of events at the expense of social, environmental, and political analyses.

Exemplary Financial Major Program

It is the position of this book that the collective restructuring of Alliance Bank, BTA Bank and Temir Bank is within the definition of a "major program." It is acknowledged that the definition of a major program is not formally defined. Nonetheless, there is an understanding that major programs are huge in scale and transformational and are in existence for many years with a temporary organizational structure. Artto, K., Martinsuo, M, et al. (2009) define a major program as having "an open system view and seek change in permanent organizations" (p.1) and program management "… as the coordinated organization, direction, and implementation of a portfolio of projects and activities that together achieve outcomes and realize benefits that are of strategic importance" (p.1).

The Restructuring Program was transformational with a complex temporary organization (Lundin and Soderholm: 1995) having to navigate the inter-equity dynamics of the various stakeholders. The banks were restructured simultaneously under the same Burden-Sharing design umbrella and approach with the same portfolio manager, the independent restructuring advisor, commandeering the program. As shown in Figure 1, the Restructuring Program had many and varied stakeholders with competing interests. Each audience of stakeholder had to be managed with differing communication strategies and guided with defined outcomes.

The organization structure was novel and transformative by vesting an independent restructuring advisor with operational control, which included devising the strategy, and process implementation. Investment banks and creditors were relegated to an execution role with government holding power over the entire process, harnessing value through the restructuring process. In essence, investment banks no longer owned the decision-making and execution value chain. They were divested of their dynamic power, modifying the business-as-usual nature of market negotiations that are inherently influenced by conflict of interest due to investment bank business models.

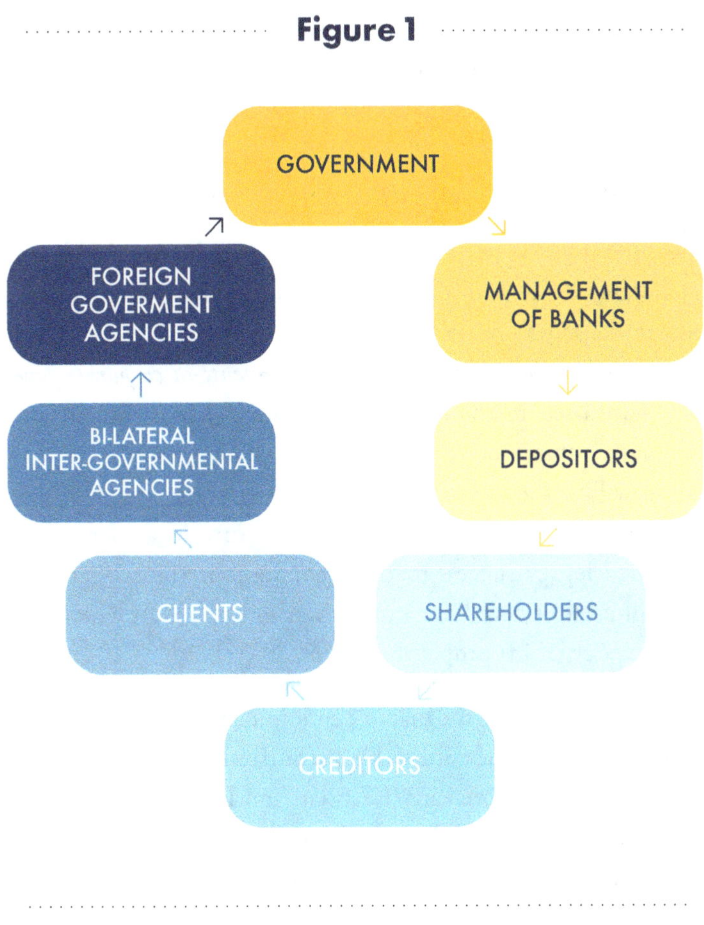

Figure 1: Multiple stakeholders of the Kazakhstan Bank Restructuring Program

Reinforcing the importance of the unique operating structure for the Burden-Sharing Restructuring Framcl Finance (IIF) publis-hed on the restructuring program stating that the success of the program was attributed to the sovereign creating its own strategy and implementing the Framework through independent advisors (IIF October 2010; p.13). The Burden-Sharing operational fra-mework challenged the modus operandi and was unequivocally of strategic importance (Artto, Martinuso., et al.) to the government of Kazakhstan seeking to preserve the fiscal profile and invest-ment grade rating of the country and support the stability of the financial system.

The pillars of the Burden-Sharing Restructuring Framework—*liquidity support, preservation of the sovereign's fiscal profile, curtailment of moral hazard, and improvements in corporate gover-nance*—are used in the book to facilitate the cross-dimensional comparative component of the analysis. Evident throughout the analysis will be the assessment of the impact of process (Davis and Thornely: 2010) and organizational structure in achieving pre-established legacy success metrics that support the program as a public interest undertaking and the tensions inherent when speed and efficiency (Ibid) propel the success.

As part of the analysis, the macro-economic impact of the Restruc-turing Program will be part of the discourse. This is a strong theme in legacy academic literature (Kasimati and Dawson: 2009) and a thread that binds the legacy effect discourse. Using the Kazakhstan Burden-Sharing Restructuring Program as a case study is relevant in unpacking the traditional major program legacy academic lite-rature and placing it within a financial major program context. In addition, for analytical plenitude, this book considers the political economy of Kazakhstan.

CHAPTER 1

FINANCIAL PORTRAIT ALONG THE SILK ROAD

*"If you are always trying to be normal, you will
never know how amazing you can be."*

—Maya Angelou, poet, civil rights activist

Kazakhstan is a land-locked, commodity-extraction-based economy, with a population of over 16 million in 2009. The tailwinds of the commodity down cycle and the financial crisis threatened the investment grade rating of the country. For a government proud of having repaid its debt to the IMF earlier than expected, incurring debt, or reversing its strong fiscal profile was not within the government's deliberation.

In the years leading to the financial crisis, commencing in 2007, Kazakhstan enjoyed many years of investor bond and equity interest, with the banks, among others, becoming prolific issuers.

I concur with a contextual summary by Principles Consultative Group in their October 2010 report: "During the decade preceding the global financial crisis, robust capital inflows helped fuel a rapid expansion in domestic credit and strong economic growth, mainly oriented in the real estate and construction sectors. As a result of this growth, Kazakh banks became more dependent on wholesale funding, which left the financial sector vulnerable to swings in international capital flows. Unsurprisingly, and in tandem with developed markets, the Kazakh banking system came under severe pressure during the global financial crisis as foreign lines of credit were interrupted, while at the same, time non-performing loans rose dramatically, and asset quality deteriorated rapidly. In addition, alleged fraudulent activities and related-party lending, often unsecured, challenged the auditors and local regulators of Alliance Bank and BTA Bank."

Research departments frequently showcased Kazakhstan as having a strong, and in some expert opinions, *the strongest*, banking systems in the CIS. I was a managing director, the head of LATAM (Latin America) and CEMEA (Central and Eastern Europe, Middle East, and Africa) corporate bond research for UBS and wrote several research reports on the Kazakhstan issuers, including the banks. I also placed many bonds in the early 2000s among diversified global investors.

Such markets and opportunities can change rapidly.

In 2008, when refinancing Eurobonds became difficult, it was revealed that the sector was over-levered and its exposure and dependency on the international capital market was a hinderance.

Faced with an international capital market suffering from illiquidity, local issuers had little alternatives for funding. The domestic deposits market was small, accounting for 44% (BTA Bank, September 2009) of funding, with the retail deposit market representing only 13% (Ibid). The sector faced huge liquidity pressure and government was concerned with the amount of external hard-currency debt issued that, according to the National Bank of

Kazakhstan, in Q1 2007, represented more than 50% of GDP. This "interconnectedness", dependency on wholesale funding and the embryonic stage of domestic capital market development, made Kazakhstan vulnerable to international financial crisis contagion.

The situation worsened for bank balance sheets when the National Bank of Kazakhstan devalued the Tenge, in February 2009, by 18%[4]. Kazakhstan was battling significant macroeconomic forces including a low commodity cycle and pressure on its international reserves emanating from the devaluation of the Russian Ruble and Ukraine Hryvnia[5]. The banking sector overexposure to real estate and non-performing loans and the slowdown of the economy, with the gross domestic product (GDP) falling to 1.2%, as reported by National Bank of Kazakhstan in October 2010, brought banking sector loan loss provisions to 30.6% by June 2009 from 5.0% in December 2006, according to BTA Bank management, with sector profits plummeting to a loss of $14.6 billion from a profit of $89 million in 2008.

This was not unusual, unfortunately. As in any financial upheaval, the crisis "depressed the prices of lower-quality investments" (Bernanke; 2001: p. 266).

Joel Motley, managing director of Public Capital Advisors, LLC, said, "Consider Timothy Geithner's book, *Stress Test*. It's very well-written, but it's scary. He's very open about the stresses he was feeling. With this gargantuan disaster in 2008-2009, we came close to bringing down the house of cards. Marcia's story is similar in the sense that Kazakhstan was dealing with managing financial

---

4 Bloomberg February 4, 2009: Kazakh Central Bank Devalues Tenge 18%, Ends Support (Update 2)

5 Bloomberg reported on 4 February 2009 that the governor of the National Bank stated that the Tenge devaluation was due to the currency pressures from Russia and Ukraine that pressured foreign currency reserves and to assist in the competitiveness of local producers.

catastrophe. She, like Geithner, brought the daring, intrepid views of a younger professional."

What were these views, and what were these options for minimizing the effects of this particularly colossal crisis? What would it take to fiscally secure the largest country of Central Asia and ninth largest in the world? Could one multi-pronged strategy integrate the breadth of expertise necessary to help save this Silk Road country?

CHAPTER 2

NO RETURN: SIX ACCEPTED STRATEGIES AND THEN, THE RIGHT ONE

At the height of the crisis, Kazakhstan was facing a loss of investor confidence with credit default swap (CDS)[6] market repricing the sovereign to historic highs of over 1600 bps, from spreads at less than 200 bps before the crisis. The widening of the spreads indicated that investors were concerned that the financial crisis and the precarious situation of the banking system could place substantial pressure on the fiscal position of the sovereign.

The work-narrative attempting to be imposed upon Kazakhstan followed six main strategies. Four of these work-narratives placed the banking sector burden on the sovereign and the other two could have exacerbated the crisis domestically:

- *Private solutions* that carried government support such as Sachsen LB's takeover by a Landesbank (IMF Country Report; July 2011) or JP Morgan, benefiting from a loan

---

6 CDS market allows investors to hedge positions by buying or selling protection. CDS may also be used as a speculative investment tool. Depending on the market CDS is more liquid than bonds.

provided by the New York Federal Reserve, acquisition of Bear Sterns (Preliminary Staff Report: 31 August 2010).

- *Direct government assistance*, which was typically affected through liquidity support provided by a sovereign to a financial institution. Global examples include Iceland, the United Kingdom, Greece, Ireland, among others (Preliminary Staff Report: 31 August 2010).

- *Emergency loans* such as the $85 billion disbursed by the U.S. government to maintain AIG solvent (Ibid) or through holding company structures utilized by Goldman Sachs and Morgan Stanley and widely reported.

- *Conservation*, which is a mechanism of transferring powers ordinarily ascribed to company directors, officers, and shareholders to a designated conservator (US Federal Housing Finance Agency) and employed to rescue Freddy Mac and Fanny Mae (Angelides and Thomas: January 2011) that were government-sponsored enterprises (GSE).

- *Emergency guarantees* that depending on the developed country, extended to liabilities other than deposits (Laeven and Valencia: 2010).

- *Bankruptcy*, with Lehman Brothers as the widely reported example of the most spectacular financial crisis and the risks involved in allowing a bank to fail in an uncontrolled manner.

These narratives did not suit the Kazakhstan government. We needed a new reality. And in Q1 2009, these strategies were publicly rejected for the adoption of a bail-in strategy that became known as the *Burden-Sharing Restructuring Framework*.

This approach, ignoring the notion of bailing out creditors, public or private, and relieving the sovereign from incurring debt, was "firstly and foremost, a political one" (Guembel and Sussman: 2009; p. 1298) with the intention of circumvented a "beggar thy neighbor" (Stiglitz; Summer 2001; p. 14) position that would place creditors' needs ahead of the country, potentially requiring the latter to adopt a post-restructuring onerous expansionary fiscal policies (Stiglitz: Summer 2001) or an austerity program. It was also controversial because Kazakhstan had room to increase its debt since the country had gross debt of only 13%, which was significantly below the 35% triple-B median (Fitch Rating, London, 20 December 2010) for an investment grade-rated sovereign.

Upon declaring the approach, government was subjected to capital-market shut-out threats and threats of being labeled a "pariah state." These scare tactics, typically levied on emerging market governments, were understood by decision-makers as a disparate attempt by creditors to use market-leverage. It was also understood that crisis breeds opportunity for investors. This is evident in the many emerging market financial crises such as the Asian, Tequila, Samba and Ruble crisis that engulfed the emerging markets throughout the late-1990s and early 2000 and saw relatively quick re-entry of investors from hedge funds to long-only participants. To engage creditors, however, government understood that the Restructuring Process needed to accurately disclose information and that the decision-making and implementation process needed to be transparent and adhere to best practice. Best practice, however, does not mean acquiescing to the impositions of the market. You can create your narrative design and implement your vision.

How transparent could a towering transformation be? Could policy and process form a perfect union? As they say, it would "take a village" and steadfast leadership.

Chronology of Key Events

May 2005	Mukhtar Ablyazov becomes Chairman of the Board of Directors of Bank TuranAlem
January 2007	Housing prices begin to fall in the US.
June 22, 2007	Bear Sterns bails out its hedge fund, which later fails.
August, 2007	Credit crisis in the US and investors leave the market.
October 2007	Standard & Poor downgraded Kazakhstan's rating to a minimum investment grade level of BBB as a result of the financial system's exposure to lending crisis.
Sept. 14, 2007	The British mortgage lender Northern Rock gets emergency loan from Bank of England.
Nov. 26, 2007	Citigroup secures capital from a $7.5 billion investment from the Abu Dhabi Investment Authority sovereign wealth fund.
2008	Bank TuranAlem rebrands itself as BTA Bank under Ablyazov's leadership.
March 16, 2008	Bear Sterns is sold to JP Morgan in a government-assisted deal.
Summer 2008	Global oil prices fall from UDS 150/bbl to USD 40bbl and cause shock in Kazakhstan.
Sept. 7, 2008	US Government rescues Fannie Mae and Freddie Mac with huge rescue package.
Sept. 15, 2008	Lehman Brothers files for bankruptcy and Merrill Lynch is sold to Bank of America.
Sept. 16, 2008	US Federal Reserve rescues AIG by buying majority shares.
October 2008	Promulgation of the Financial Stabilization Law in Kazakhstan.
December 31, 2008	Ernst & Young report outlines deteriorating financial profile and looming insolvency for BTA bank.
February 2009	The Agency of the Republic of Kazakhstan on Regulation and Supervision of Financial Market and Financial Organizations (the "FMSA") offers to purchase majority interest in BTA Bank JSC.
February 2009	Following devaluations in Russia and the Ukraine, the tenge was devalued to improve the competitiveness of Kazakh exports.
February 9, 2009	Marcia Favale-Tarter meets with Grigory Marchenko and Kairat Kelimbetov.

*Source: Oxford University-Said Business School, 2015, Case
Study by Ansar, Atif and Ariell Ahearn (25 May 2015); Banking
Sector Restructuring Program in Kazakhstan-BTA Bank JSC*

CHAPTER 3

RISE TO TRANSFORMATION

AS THE BANKS began to report large balance sheet impairment, government was concerned by the lack of visibility of the extent of the balance sheet weakness. Insolvency values were fluctuating by the day. Alexander (1997) captured this dynamic in his statement; "the net worth of a problem bank with an impaired loan portfolio can only be estimated and will evolve as the underlying circumstances of the economy and bank's clients change and as asset values shift, partly in response to changes in public confidence and economic policies" (p. 3).

Government knew that public and investor confidence needed to be restored. As a result, Kazakhstan committed to a series of meaningful steps. Namely, Kazakhstan acted with expediency, elaborating and implementing most key transformative decisions within an eighteen-month period—the speed and efficiency of which is arguably enhanced by the political economy of the country. On 23 October 2008, government enacted the Financial Stabilization Law "aimed at strengthening the stability and resilience of the country's financial system. The law also aimed at strengthening the position of the country's financial authority" (IIF; October 2010; p.13). In Q1 2009, government provided $10 billion Anti-Crisis Plan money to assist the real economy and the financial sector[7]. The financial sector was allocated $4 billion to "establish new or revive old channels of credit flow after a major disruption and to rehabilitate insolvent debtors" (Bernanke 2001: p. 272).

To increase liquidity in the system, the National Bank of Kazakhstan, under the astute leadership of Grigori Marchenko, did its part by lowering reserve requirements to 0%, for the restructuring banks, and by providing repo lines, and by re-defining accepted collateral. To avert bank runs that "… are a common feature of the extreme crisis that have played a prominent role in monetary history" (Diamond and Dybvig 1983; p. 401), the National Bank increased retail deposit insurance and extended the deposit-insurance to 99% of the population. As a further measure to maintain liquidity, within targeted banks, government-owned companies were directed to maintain deposits at specific banks. I was directly involved in the elaboration and successful implementation of this policy.

In Q1 2009, when auditors completed their review of the banks and recapitalization needs determined, government began the Burden-Sharing Restructuring Program selecting Alliance Bank, BTA Bank, and Temir Bank as participants. Government had already intervened in the first two banks and the third was of interest because it was a leading mortgage lender. The three banks were meaningful to the banking system overall, representing the first, fifth and sixth largest banks in total assets.

The banks were restructured simultaneously under the same Burden-Sharing Restructuring Program umbrella design approach with the same portfolio manager commandeering the program. Each of the banks had the same restructuring design. All three examples required creditor and government sharing the burden of recapitalizing the banks, with substantial haircuts being imposed on the creditors.

---

7 Kazinform

Summary of Restructuring Terms

Alliance Bank Restructuring Outcome

The Bank had total recapitalization needs of $3.6 billion and total eligible debt of $5.3 billion. Creditors provided $2.7 billion as equity through debt cancellation and bond conversion into equity. This post-restructuring outstanding amount was available to creditors through four security options based on eligibility. In addition, creditors were provided Recovery Notes to participate in balance sheet improvements from asset recovery management. Total amount of creditor exposure before conversion was $4.4 billion, implying a 61% haircut in principal value. Government, through the sovereign welfare fund, Samruk-Kazyna, contributed $860 million in equity by converting all debt owed into equity.

BTA Bank Summary of Restructuring Outcome

The Bank had total recapitalization needs of $11.256 billion and total eligible debt of $16.7 billion. Creditors provided $6.8 billion as equity through debt cancellation and bond conversion into equity. This post-restructuring outstanding amount was available to creditors through five security options based on eligibility. In addition, creditors were provided Recovery Notes to participate in balance sheet improvements from asset recovery management. Total amount of creditor exposure before conversion was $12.2 billion, implying a 56% haircut in principal value. Government, through the sovereign welfare fund, Samruk-Kazyna, contributed $4.45 billion equity by converting all debt owed into equity.

Temir Bank Summary of Restructuring Outcome

The Bank had total recapitalization needs of $804 million and total eligible debt of $1.4 billion. Creditors provided $650 million as equity through debt cancellation and bond conversion into equity.

This post-restructuring outstanding amount was available to creditors through four security options based on eligibility. Total amount of creditor exposure before conversion was $1.4 billion implying a 46% haircut in principal value. Government, through the sovereign welfare fund, Samruk-Kazyna, contributed $154 million in equity.

Making the Right Changes

The process began in an organized manner and announced to the public when I was designated as the independent restructuring advisor, given the de facto project manager role and then, made a senior advisor to the prime minister of Kazakhstan, Karim Massimov. The role required devising the restructuring strategy and executing the restructuring program. This operational structure required investment banks, global law firms and accounting firms, to de facto report to me on behalf of government and the banks themselves.

This operational structure debunked the importance of the global investment bank-centric model. Investment banks, although important, were not leading and deciding i.e. they did not call the shots relegating all else to a secondary supporting role. Therefore, the structure re-directed control of the entire process to government through the independent advisor i.e. project manager, eliminating conflicts of interest and providing greater strategic flexibility and enforceability[8]. The impact of this operational structure was recognized by IIF (2010) that stated:

"From the onset of the restructuring process, while devising its own appropriate restructuring strategy, the

---

8 Author presented report, "Terra Incognita"; 29 January 2010 and to the "Weathering the Financial Storm" October 2010 Presentation; presented at Oxford; Distinguished Speaker Series for a further discussion and analysis of the Kazakhstan Bank Restructuring.

government of Kazakhstan stated its commitment to best market-based restructuring practice in accordance with the principles. In February 2009, the government hired independent advisors who provided restructuring and asset recovery advice that served to form the restructuring strategy and framework, which was a burden-sharing approach that excluded the provision of guarantees while ensuring the banks' ongoing operations and, in the case of BTA Bank, the asset recovery framework committing the bank and its shareholders to undertake legal action to realize value for the banks and their creditors." (p.13)

The next definitive step was when the government adopted, in Q1 2009, the Law on Introduction of Amendments and Additions to Certain Legislative Acts of the Republic of Kazakhstan on the issues of Perfecting the Legislation of the Republic of Kazakhstan on Money Payments and Transfers, Accounting and Financial Reporting of Financial Organizations, Banking Activities and the Activities of the National Bank of the Republic of Kazakhstan (Restructuring Law), which I advocated for and championed.

"Among other things, the Law amends the Law of the Republic of Kazakhstan on Banks and Banking Activity. These amendments establish a procedure for restructuring of a bank, which can be held to be binding upon its creditors including a dissenting minority of those creditors" (Denton Wilde Sapte; July 2009, p.1).

Having commissioned the law, The Restructuring Law was written with the intention to be compatible with United Nations Commission on International Trade Law (UNCITRAL) Model Insolvency Law. Furthering the importance of harmonization, I was invited by the E15 committee to participate and provide a written contribution to the World Economic Forum proposing the adoption of a unified restructuring laws for the emerging markets. The contribution advocates simplification of restructuring processes in the emerging markets to include a Model Law.

"The Model Law is designed to assist States to equip their insolvency laws with a modern legal framework to more effectively address cross-border insolvency proceedings concerning debtors experiencing severe financial distress or insolvency. It focuses on authorizing and encouraging cooperation and coordination between jurisdictions, rather than attempting the unification of substantive insolvency law and respects the differences among national procedural laws. For the purposes of the Model Law, a cross-border insolvency is one where the insolvent debtor has assets in more than one State or where some of the creditors of the debtor are not from the State where the insolvency proceeding is taking place"[9]

Lastly, government waved taxes on the debt reduction to alleviate liquidity pressures on the banks. These forgone taxes amounted to a form of restructuring subsidy. To recuperate the support provided, the restructuring strategy envisioned privatization of these banks, with the intent that Samruk-Kazyna, the sovereign welfare fund, would divest its majority ownership of the three banks, at a profit. Ultimately, government merged Alliance Bank and Temir Bank (2014) under new ownership and BTA Bank (2014) under Kazkommertsbank.

Finance can be elusive. Who were my partners over the course of this tremendous venture? What were the tenants of this innovative major program? Can other countries follow? Let's dive deeper into the fundamentals of the program.

---

9 (UNCITRAL; https://uncitral.un.org/en/texts/insolvency/modellaw/cross-border_insolvency

CHAPTER 4

FUNDAMENTALS OF THE BURDEN-SHARING RESTRUCTURING PROGRAM

UNDER A "CONFIDENTIAL" classification, WikiLeaks reported: "On August 8, 2009, Prime Minister Karim Masimov briefed a U.S. Congressional delegation led by House Minority Leader John Boehner (R-OH) on a wide range of economic and energy issues. ...Rep. Walden (R-OR) asked the Prime Minister if the government had an exit strategy for the financial crisis. In response, he said, "I thought you would ask me about that!" turned to his left, and summoned to the table Marcia Favale-Tarter, a Western banking advisor who owns her own consulting firm and regularly advises the Prime Minister and the Chairman of National Welfare Fund Samruk-Kazyna, Kairat Kelimbetov. Favale-Tarter, who clearly has the Prime Minister's confidence, explained the government's plans to the delegation."

Here begins the discussion of the objectives of the Restructuring Program and sets the framework in answering to what extent the Burden-Sharing Restructuring Program created legacy effects in Kazakhstan. One of the core principles of the Burden-Sharing restructuring was to bail-in creditors and engage them as 'partners in the process' of restructuring the banks. Government was keen on having management teams of the banks gain operational knowledge from investors that would improve operations. Moreover, government was not pre-disposed to bail-out professional investors and shift their risk exposure to government, relieving investors from investment responsibility and bank management from direct accountability.

The restructuring strategy identified four pillars as essential to establish the banks as going concerns, whilst preserving the fiscal strength of the country. See Figure 2 below.

Intertwined in each was the intent of creating a positive perception of Kazakhstan. These pillars were:

- liquidity support
- preservation of the sovereign's fiscal profile
- curtailment of moral hazard
- improvement in corporate governance

Figure 2

Figure 2: Four Pillars of Restructuring Strategy

Liquidity Support

The driving principle for this category was to ensure that funds provided to the bank were used to sustain the operations of the bank rather than being funneled to creditors. By re-directing liquidity, the banks were able to meet ATM and retail deposits/withdrawals, assuaging fears of an imminent collapse of the banks. This measure helped to prevent or minimize a run on the banks and adhered to the domestic legislation that had a "watershed" approach to the priority of payment of a bankrupt Kazakhstan domiciled bank. Priority of payment was as follows: "(a) administrative and legal expenses of the bankruptcy, (b) payments for tort claims involving harm to life or health, (c) payments due to employees as a result of "their employment and related social security and mandatory pension payments, (d) the deposit insurance organization's claims related to insured deposits, (e) claims of individual depositors relating to deposits and transfers, (f) deposits made from pension fund assets and deposits of life insurance companies, (g) claims of non-for-profit organizations, (h) secured creditors of the bank, (i) tax liability settlements and repayment of borrowings from the state budget, and (j) unsecured claims of creditors, subordinated unsecured claims" (White & Case; slide 8). In essence, this objective not only adhered to legislation but also challenged the self-serving notion that best market practice meant placing creditors ahead of others in the priority of payment.

As I told *Financial Times* (FT) on October 6, 2009, "It is a major step in the restructuring for Alliance and for the system as it is the first bank to restructure as a going concern without introducing conservation [taking it into state control]."

"I don't believe what we are trying to achieve in Kazakhstan in terms of restructuring the debt of a bank on the basis it emerges as a going concern, has been done anywhere else in the world," said Francis Fitzherbert-Brockholes, partner at White & Case, in the same *FT* piece.

Preserving Sovereign's Fiscal Profile

Kazakhstan is economically highly dependent on commodities with crude petroleum in 2008 accounting for over 50% of total exports[10]. The financial crisis, coupled with the decline in commodity prices, combined to pressure GDP growth with the growth rate plummeting to less than 3% in 2008 from double-digit growth in the years 2004-2007[11]. At the time, the sovereign was rated investment grade, which carries a direct impact on the cost of funding in the country and for all domestic issuers. Losing the investment grade rating would pressure the entire economic-value-chain by pushing the cost of borrowing substantially higher for all issuers—whilst tarnishing the perception of Kazakhstan as an investment destination. Therefore, preserving the rating was of paramount concern.

Moral Hazard

The Burden-Sharing framework was designed to curtail the risk of Moral Hazard. "Financial regulators have a legitimate interest in intervening when somebody takes a risk that then causes a further risk for others in the financial system. This externality means that overall risk-taking may be excessive" (Dow; December 2000: p. 2) and "…that initial shocks can be multiplied inside the firm by moral hazard and financial leverage, so that an individual firm may deliver a large shock to the financial system" (p. 3). Kazakhstan was already grappling with the top four banks in terms of total asset value having insolvency concerns given poor loan management and alleged fraudulent corporate activity. If the government took its support to the level advocated by international creditors (bail-out), creditors and managements would be relieved of their investment and governance responsibilities.

---

10 Observatory of Economic Complexity

11 World Bank, World Development Indicators

Dissuasion was key to success. The writing of a blank check either through a sovereign guarantee, direct loan or a private-to-public bond exchange could encourage other banks to seek the same remedy for their excessive risk-taking.

Corporate Governance

This pillar established the notion that creditor involvement enhanced corporate governance by retaining the creditors as *'partners in the process'*, a phrase I coined within the narrative design of the Burden-Sharing Framework, through their residual ownership in the banks via equity and debt. Each restructuring offered a combination of debt with a minority equity-ownership in the banks. Since a key concern of creditors was the state of the non-performing loans in the banks, the restructuring terms included asset recovery notes. These instruments derived value against a pool of non-performing loans.

Proper management for value creation was needed to prevent further alleged corporate abuses, fraud, and general mismanagement. To strengthen the governance and therefore management of the same, the corporate charters were re-written providing extraordinary powers of veto to the creditors for key management topics such as loan approvals and oversight over the asset recovery process from where the creditors through the asset recovery notes gained the ability to participate in the upside of non-performing loans' value-recovery. The charters were also amended for creditors' director positions on the board of directors by creditor directors. These creditor directors were independent and accountable to note holders. These creditor directors chaired strategic committees including *Auditing, Asset Recovery* and *Governance*.

Transparency and Disclosure

Transparency and disclosure were fundamental to the restructuring process. For the Burden-Sharing Restructuring program to be implemented successfully creditors and the larger investment universe needed to be persuaded that the restructuring process adhered to best practice. Moreover, the Restructuring Law required an *all-creditor vote*, which meant two-thirds of the creditor base had to vote in favor of the restructuring terms for the restructuring to be approved and binding. For this objective to be met, the restructuring process would need to provide accurate disclosure.

To this end, all three banks created a reinforcing mechanism through the steering committee structure representing one-third of all outstanding debt. Its composition included trade finance, ECA, hedge funds and commercial banks, excluding domestic bank. These committees were structured to include the different classes of debt with the intent of creating inter-equity tension that would benefit the banks during the restructuring negotiations. Once a recapitalization amount was agreed, through a process of balance sheet evaluation and business plan verification, Samruk-Kazyna would allocate its participation—leaving the remaining recapitalization to be negotiated among the debt holders.

This tactic relieved the sovereign from assuming the entirety of the debt burden whilst placing the details of the restructuring haircut to be decided by the debt participants. The structure was unusual because it caused inter-equity dynamics, which meant negotiation pressure was internalized amongst the creditor groups rather than focusing the entire negotiation exercise against government or bank management.

The banks went on roadshows to garner creditor support with the steering committees vocally supporting the deals. As the independent restructuring advisor and senior advisor to the prime minister, I personally took part in roadshows and in steering committee meetings, negotiating directly with the creditors and communicating directly with government, bank managements and the team of advisors from both sides. All three of the banks, Alliance Bank, BTA Bank and Temir Bank, received over 90% creditor approval for each of the three banks. Immediately thereafter, the restructuring was approved by local courts and recognized by jurisdictions that were members of UNICTRAL or recognized Model Insolvency.

Below is a detailed breakdown of each bank's steering committee participants.

- **Alliance Bank** steering committee members: Asian Development Bank; Credit Agricole Corporate and Investment Bank; Commerzbank Aktiengesellschaft; DEG—Deutsche Investitions—und Entwicklungsgesellschaft mbH; HSBC Bank plc; Bank of Singapore Limited; JPMorgan Chase Bank, N.A.; Sumitomo Mitsui Banking Corporation Europe Limited; and Wells Fargo Bank, National Association. (Source: Alliance Bank 2009 Management Presentation)

- **BTA Bank** committee members: Bank of Singapore Limited; Commerzbank Aktiengesellschaft; D. E. Shaw Group; DEG—Deutsche Investitions—und Entwicklungsgesellschaft mbH; Euler Hermes; Fortis Investment; Gramercy Advisors LLC; Standard Chartered Bank; The Royal Bank of Scotland; US Ex-Im Bank; and Wells Fargo Bank, National Association. (Source: BTA Bank September 2009 Management Presentation)

- **Temir Bank** committee members: Banco Finantia International Limited, Black River Emerging Markets

Credit Fund Ltd, BTG Absolute Return Master Fund LP, Nomura International plc, and Portland Worldwide Investments Limited. (Source: Temir Bank 2009 Management Presentation)

Legacy Effects and Money Modernization

The challenge in this analysis is that legacy itself is vague and that academic literature in major programs have not considered in-depth and within the academic-framework-discussion the legacy effects borne from financial major programs. In answering to what extent the Restructuring Program created legacy effects, this section draws parallels from other "major program" events in addressing this academic. Correspondingly, this section, analyzes the legacy effects through the definition, "legacy can cover many different aspects including image, economics, built environment, and sustainability" (Davis and Thornley, pg. 89) and unpacks this definition within the context of the objectives of the Burden-Sharing Restructuring Program.

Moral Hazard

Curtailing moral hazard was a key component of adopting the Burden-Sharing restructuring framework. There was a risk of the external financial crisis creating an environment for systemic risk[12] within the Kazakhstan banking through moral hazard's potential impact on the financial system (Dow; December 2000). As argued by Dow (2000) moral hazard's contribution to systemic

---

12 Dow, James (December 2000 the author discusses moral hazard as a "key element of systemic risk" (p.1). The book recognizes that there is no "universally recognized definition of systematic risk" (p.2) and discusses the different notions of systemic risk for the financial system and its importance to policymakers. It does, however, advocate that moral hazard is potentially impacting within the systemic risk context.

risk is a justifiable concern to central banks. Dow (2000) parts from the notion that "…systemic risk, being a matter of public policy, should refer to cases of risks being imposed on the financial system where some element of externality exists. In other words, financial regulators have a legitimate interest in intervening when somebody takes a risk that then causes a further risk for others in the financial system. This externality means that overall risk-taking may be excessive" (Dow; December 2000; p.2).

Externalities existed.

The liquidity crunch caused by the seizure of the international capital market placed pressure on balance sheets. Issuers did not have a ready market to refinance risk and finance non-performing loans. Moreover, government intervened in the four top banks that received direct support, whereby accountability for potential governance misdeeds, except for BTA Bank, were not entirely made public. I was directly involved in the deliberation of transferring the BTA Bank fraud case to the English courts. According to BTA Bank management, the estimated amount of alleged fraud involved assets within the range of $5 billion to $8 billion. The BTA Bank case was covered by numerous news sources between 2009 and 2011 regarding the former chairman being pursued by authorities for corporate fraud. Asset recovery took a life of its own with John Howell as the independent advisor, bringing the overall restructuring value above $30 billion.

Government needed to dissuade bank managements from abandoning corporate responsibility and latch onto the external bail-out frameworks that would relieve accountability. The fear was that the lack of corporate responsibility manifest in Alliance Bank and even Temir Bank and BTA Bank would cause a knock-on restructuring effect to mask incompetence or fraud[13].

____

13 (29 January 2010) Terra Incognita paper written by the author. The report addresses the benefits and determent of related party lending as well as the

In terms of this distinct legacy effect, government was successful in curtailing moral hazard. The restructuring rhetoric was contained to only the three banks: Alliance Bank, BTA Bank and Temir Bank. Domestic confidence re-engaged. Massive and sustained bank deposit-runs were averted. The chairmen of both Alliance Bank and BTA Bank were responding to domestic, and in the case of BTA Bank, international, charges of criminal conduct. Management teams of other banks took note.

Lastly, government took the opportunity to strengthen regulatory powers of the financial banking authorities.

Upstanding Image

Nation-branding is an important aspect of building sovereign profiles. It has a direct influence on foreign and domestic investment perception. The perception, therefore, of Kazakhstan during the turbulent financial crisis was a key aspect when considering the controversial Burden-Sharing framework. Integral to the concept of place or nation branding is to accept that product "is anything that can be offered to a market for attention, acquisition, use or consumption that might satisfy a want or need. It includes physical objects, services, persons, places, organizations, and ideas (Kotler et al. 2008; P. 500)". Following the definition by Kotler et al., "Investors must perceive Kazakhstan and its banking sectors as a value proposition when compared to other emerging and even developed markets. If one accepts that Kazakhstan and correspondingly, the banking sector, are products, then country and sector can be branded." Kazakhstan needed to be the branded

---

organizational structure at BTA that allowed for corporate abuses and fraud. The lending practice and corporate structure analyzed was not abnormal in the Kazakhstan financial system. The author also wrote a paper (30 November 2009) titled, Alliance Bank: Fraud in the Steppe.

organization, in accordance with Aaker's (2006) argument that the brand equity of the organization (i.e., nation) is a determinant of the product (banking sector) value proposition.

Government spent a considerable amount of time and resources to promote the Burden-Sharing Restructuring through media[14] and through the annual Astana Forums that bring together world leaders and policy experts, along with other venues receiving favorable and laudatory remarks from various experts. I spoke at various government-sponsored events, including on "CNBC World Report: Special on Kazakhstan" and gave numerous interviews providing a unified message i.e. controlling the narrative design and the visibility of the Restructuring Program. Kazakhstan was intent on being perceived as a responsible market participant, forging a path of issuer independence within best market practices, which they achieved.

Operating Environment and Corporate Governance

The Burden-Sharing Restructuring served to improve the built environment; whereby the built environment is adapted to the operational environment in keeping with the definition "the term. *built environment*, is used when referring to those surroundings created for humans, by humans, and to be used for human activity"[15].

The Board of Directors was revamped with creditor representatives serving on the board. Charters were re-formulated reinforcing the

---

14 Interview with Prime Minster of Kazakhstan and author: *CNBC World Report Special* on Kazakhstan, that outlined the initially controversial but successful Kazakh Burden-Sharing restructuring (March 2011)

15 University of Windsor;
https://www.uwindsor.ca/vabe/25/what-does-term-"built-environment"-mean

rights of creditor, allowing for key oversight and veto power. These reinforcements in instances were drafted beyond the reach of the joint-stock Kazakhstan regulation. Many of the precepts were adopted into regulation such as greater board oversight in credit lending and the requirement of reporting on off-balance sheet activities to financial authority regulators including the National Bank of Kazakhstan.

As a by-product of the Restructuring Program, Kazakhstan created a key legacy effect by adopting the Restructuring Law, which has been subsequently amended to include all corporate issuers. The argument being that centrality of laws add to the value of a company and protects from self-dealing transactions (McCahery, Moerland, et al.; 2002: p.7), which in turn, improves corporate governance.

This is an important outcome because self-dealing was apparent in BTA Bank and Alliance Bank, and not an isolated factor within the Kazakhstan banking sector, contributing to their insolvency. Improvements in curtailing this practice had direct value-creating implications for the system and the perception of the country.

Macroeconomic Impact and Sovereign Profile

A common thread of the legacy effect narrative among academics is the macroeconomic impact of a major or mega event. This legacy effect was of paramount importance in the elaboration of the Restructuring Program. Government was concerned with the fiscal profile and in maintaining the sovereign rating and in justifying to the domestic public that its policy would positively impact the economy. To that end, the National Bank governor, at Oxford, in October 2010, presented on the impact declaring the Restructuring Program a success as viewed through five indicators.

The first indicator provides a gauge of banking system health through payment flows. For the period October 2008-2010, there was a 10.9% increase in the volume of payment signaling a returned of confidence in the system. The second indicator was the external liabilities of the banking system. These were reduced by KZT[16] 2.8 TG billion[17], thus alleviating balance sheet pressures borne from exchange rate fluctuations and onerous debt levels. The third indicator focused on the liquidity of the banking sector, as a percent of total assets. This indicator grew from 14% in September-2008 to 24.7% September-2010. The fourth indicator inflation collapsed to 6.5% (2010) from 20% (2008). The fifth indicator, the National Bank liabilities, grew to KZT832.2 TG billion in September 2010 due to outstanding support adjusting to KZT 723.2 TG billion by October 2010.

Based on these positive macroeconomic indicators, government was able to maintain its investment grade rating by the three leading rating agencies: Moody's, Standard & Poor's, and Fitch. Given that rating changes have an almost immediate impact on the sovereign cost of funding and therefore the base rate for all issuers within the country, preservation of an investment grade rating is a priority for governments.

16 KZT = Kazakhstani Tenge

17 (Exchange rate at 1 KZT = USD 0.0069 October 2010) Exchange rate.org. uk http:// www.exchangerates.org.uk/KZT-USD-14_10_2010-exchange-rate-history.html

CHAPTER 5

SUSTAINABLE EMPOWERMENT

FINANCIAL CRISES ARE becoming more impactful, given the interconnectivity of markets and participants. Cross-border funding and the globalized structure of economic growth, places crises within the realm of inter-country policy considerations. Hence, the importance of understanding the legacy effects of mega-projects and meaningful impact on the population of a country, stakeholders, and policymakers.

Returning to the original question, Kazakhstan achieved legacy effects as defined by the Restructuring Program. Government was able to curtail moral hazard and preserve the fiscal profile. Given the success in implementing the Restructuring Program, Kazakhstan neither issued sovereign debt nor suffered an investment grade rating downgrade. The country neither turned into a pariah state nor suffered an investor shut-out from capital markets. Rather, amid the restructuring, in May 2010, Kazatomprom, a government-owned entity, issued a $500 million five-year Eurobonds at a coupon rate of 6.25%[18], a historic low.

---

18 Kazatomprom: https://kazatomprom.kz/en/page/istoriya_kompanii

The banking system did not collapse. Creditors remained participants in the banks transferring corporate governance knowledge
and expertise. Kazakhstan was able to brand its investment image,
improve its economic profile, reformulate the operational envi-
ronments for banks with management buy-in and strengthen the
banking sector through targeted rule-based modifications.

From the perspective of policy and decision makers there are three
main legacy effect and academic takeaways to be further explored beyond the discussion of the objectives of the Restructuring
Program. These include the role of law in advancing corporate
governance, regulatory legacy effects and the importance of the
political-economy construct of Kazakhstan in the process-success
of the Burden-Sharing Restructuring Program.

The first is within the legacy effects of corporate governance and
the discourse that the structure of capital markets and a country's
corporate governance are influenced by law (Skeel Jnr, D.A. 2004)
and that markets that display strong minority investor protection
encourage a more diverse and dispersed ownership structure (La
Porta, Lopez-de-Silanes, et al.: 1998)[19]. By passing the Restructuring Law, Kazakhstan took an instrumental step in harmonizing
its legal structure with world best practices and in placing the
sovereign as a responsible participant within the globalized financial markets.

The second is regulatory legacy effects (Moloney, Niamh; Chapter
2; 2012). Kazakhstan began an exercise of driving board level
corporate governance improvements through charter modifica-
tion and through retaining investors as partners in the process

---

19 R. La Porta, F. Lopez-de-Silanes, A. Shleifer, and R. Vishny, (1998) "Law and
finance," Journal of Political Economy, 106, 1113–55; R. La Porta, F. Lopez-
de-Silanes and A. Shleifer, "Corporate ownership around the world," Journal of
Finance, 54 (1999), 471–517. For a further discussion.

of restructuring the banks. The success was dependent on all participants exercising their responsibilities. The initiative then transpired to strengthening the regulatory bodies oversight of the banks through a series of rule-based modifications.

The third introduces the political economy[20] of Kazakhstan, as well as its culture, as a contributing factor to process success. This is an area to be explored further by major program academic studies. Kazakhstan benefited from the President-centric model given his influence over the Legislative, Judiciary and Executive powers. Controversial policies were able to be exacted without worry of the electoral mechanisms (Persson and Tabellini: 2000) exerting power over decisions. This power-centric structure allowed for speed and efficiency in the Restructuring Program process to balance amicable without interfering spheres of political interests.

A Call to Academics Within the Major Program Management Field of Study

The importance—and universality—of the Kazakhstan Restructuring Program is that it allowed for a framework to unbundle legacy effects and concepts within the major program management discourse and apply these to a major program within the financial universe. In keeping with the intent of this case study, which was to elevate the discourse from global sporting events and infrastructure and to encourage policymakers and practitioners to evaluate legacy effects when elaborating any major financial programs, the book concludes with the recommendation that major

---

20 Persson, T. and Guido Tabellini (2000) Political economy literature focus mainly on developed democracies and therefore, the median voter is a policy driver. Kazakhstan is different given that the country has been governed by the same President since its independence who has substantial powers of influence.

financial programs need to adhere to a system design (*operational structure*) that enables legacy effects that are measurable and attainable within the timeframe of the sitting government. To that end, governments need to be able to have transformative, temporary organizations to enhance performance and be mindful of the political construct, which, if well-managed, improves process efficiency and deepens the discourse underpinning the project.

REFERENCES

Aaker, David A. (2006); Building Strong Brands; The Free Press

Alexander, W. (1997) Systemic Bank Restructuring & Macroeconomic Polices: International Monetary Fund

Alliance Bank, 2009 Management Presentation

Angelides, Phil, and Bill Thomas. (January 2011) 'The Financial Crisis Inquiry Report: Final Report of the National Commission on the Causes of the Financial Crisis and Economic Crisis in the United States', The Financial Crisis Inquiry Commission: Government Printing Office.

Ansar, Atif and Ariell Ahearn (25 May 2015); Banking Sector Restructuring Program in Kazakhstan-BTA Bank JSC; Oxford University

Artto, K., Martinuso, M., Gemünden, HG. and Murauro, J. (2009), 'Foundations of program management: A bibliometric view', *International Journal of Project Management*, 27(1): 1-18.

Bernanke, B.S. (2001): "Nonmonetary Effects of the Financial Crisis in the Propagation of the Great Depression," *The American Economic Review*, 73 (3), pp. 257-277.

BTA Bank Management September 2009 Presentation

Bloomberg, February 4, 2009 (Nariman Gizitdinov): Kazakh Central Bank Devalues Tenge 18%, Ends Support (Update

2): http://www.bloomberg.com/apps/news? pid=newsarchive&refer=home&sid=aROyGJTxpQbA; Accessed 28 June 2015

Club de Paris. Conference on Sustainable Financing of Emerging and Developing Countries. June 16, 2010. https://clubdeparis.org/en/communications/page/conference-on-sustainable-financing-of-emerging-and-developing-countries

Corporate Live Wire. "BTA Bank Successfully Completed Restructuring Of Financial Debt For The Amount Of $11.1 Billion." *Corporate Live Wire*. March 26, 2013. https://corporatelivewire.com/deal.html?id=bta-bank-successfully-completed-restructuring-of-financial-debt-for-the-amount-of-111-billion

Davis, Juliet, and Andy Thornely (2010): Urban regeneration for the London 2012 Olympics: Issues of land acquisition and legacy; Cities Programme, London School of Economics, United Kingdom; Department of Geography, London School of Economics, United Kingdom; City, Culture and Society 1 89–98

Denton Wilde Sapte (July 2009): Memorandum to the Steering Committee

Diamond, D.W. and Dybvig, P.H. (1983) "Bank runs, deposit insurance, and liquidity", Journal of Political Economy, 91 (3), pp. 401-419.

Dow, James (December 2000): Monetary and Economic Studies; "What Is Systemic Risk? Moral Hazard, Initial Shocks, and Propagation"

Exchange rate.org.uk http://www.exchangerates.org.uk/KZT-USD-14_10_2010-ex- change-rate-history.html; Accessed 4 August 2015

Favale, Marcia, (30 November 2009) Alliance Bank: "Fraud in the Steppe"

___. (29 January 2010) "Terra Incognita"

___. (2010); "Breaking the Mold." *Paris Club Annual Report.*

___. (27 September 2010) Marketing Assignment

___. (October 2010); Presentation: "Weathering the Financial Storm," Distinguished Speaker Series; University of Oxford

___. (January 2011); Presentation to the World Bank

Ferran, Eilís; Niamh Moloney, Jennifer G. Hill and John C. Coffee, Jr (2012) ; The Regulatory Aftermath of the Global Financial Crisis Book DOI: http://dx.doi.org/ 10.1017/ CBO9781139175821; Moloney, Niamh; Chapter 2 - The legacy effects of the financial crisis on regulatory design in the EU; pp 111-202; Chapter DOI: http://dx.- doi.org/10.1017/ CBO9781139175821.004 Cambridge University Press; accessed 5 August 2015

Fitch Rating London 20 December 2010

Gold, J., & Gold, M. (2008). 'Riding the Mexican Wave? Deciphering the meaning of Olympic Legacy'. In Proceedings of the Conference on The Olympic Legacy: People, Place and Enterprise, University of Greenwich, May 8/9.

Guembel, A., and Oren Sussman (2009); "Sovereign Debt without Default Penalties," *Review of Economic Studies* 76, 1297–1320

Hall, C., & Hodges, J. (1996). "The party's great, but what about the hangover? The housing and social impacts of mega-events with special reference to the 2000: Sydney Olympics."

Kasimati, Evangelia and Peter Dawson (2009), "Assessing the impact of the 2004 Olympic Games on the Greek economy: A small macroeconomic model; economic Modeling 26; 139-146"

Kazatomprom: http://www.kazatomprom.kz/en/#!/node/111, accessed 2 September 2015),

Kazakhstan Heart of Eurasia (January 2011) Presentation

Kazinform: http://en.government.kz/site/news/112008/05; Accessed 26 January 2010

Kotler, Philip; Armstrong, Gary; Wong, Veronica; Saunders, John. (2008), *Principles of Marketing*; 5th European edition; Pearson Education Limited

IMF Country Report. (July 2011) "Germany: Technical Note on Crisis Management Arrangements," Report No. 11/368, https://www.imf.org/external/pubs/cat/longres.aspx?sk=25458.0, Accessed 27 July 2015.

"IMF Kazakhstan Repays the IMF Ahead of Schedule," https://www.imf.org/external/ np/sec/nb/2000/nb0035.htm; accessed 30 August 2015

Institute of International Finance (IIF) (October 2010): "Principles for Stable Capital Flows and Fair Debt Restructuring," *Report on Implementation by the Principles Consultative Group*

Laeven, Luc, & Fabian Valencia. (2010) "Resolution of Banking Crisis: The Good, the Bad, the Ugly." International Monetary Fund.

La Porta, R., F. Lopez-de-Silanes, A. Shleifer, and R. Vishny, (2009) "Law and finance," Journal of Political Economy, 106 (1998), 1113–55; R. La Porta, F. Lopez-de-Silanes and A. Shleifer, "Corporate ownership around the world," *Journal of Finance*, 54, 471–517

Lazard (2010) Internal Presentation to BTA Bank Management

Lundin, Rolf A., and Anders Soderholm (1995) A theory of the temporary organization: Scand. J. Mgmt., Vol.11 No. 4, pp 437-455

McCahery, Joseph, A, Piet Moerland, Theo Raaijmakers, Luc Renneboog (2002): Corporate Governance Regimes; Convergence and Diversity; Oxford University Press.

Minnaert, Lynn (2011): "An Olympic legacy for all? The non-infrastructural outcomes of the Olympic Games for socially excluded groups" (Atlanta 1996-Beijing 2008); *JTMA*; Article 2180

National Bank of Kazakhstan (October 2010) Presentation: "The experience of restructuring banks' external debt in Kazakhstan"

Observatory of Economic Complexity. http://atlas.media.mit.edu/explore/tree/_map/ hs/export/kaz/all/show/2008/Accessed 2 August 2014

Persson, T & Guido Tabellini (2000); Political Economics: Explaining Economic Policy; Massachusetts Institute of Technology

Preliminary Staff Report (31 August 2010): Government Rescues of "too-big-to-fail" financial institutions', Financial Crisis Inquiry Commission, http://fcic-static.law.stan- ford.edu/cdn_media/fcic-reports/2010-0831-Governmental-Rescues.pdf, Accessed 27 July 2015.

Reuters (Raushan Nurshayeva); 15 June 2010 2:56 am EDT: http://www.reuters.com/ article/2010/06/15/us-kazakhstan-president-idUSTRE65E0WP20100615; Accessed 26 June 2015

Sakoui, Anousha, Gillian Tett, and Isabel Gorst. "Kazakhstan secures Alliance Bank restructuring." *Financial Times*. October 6, 2009.

https://www.ft.com/content/30f85b26-b29f-11de-b7d2-00144feab49a

Skeel Jnr., D. A. (2004), "Corporate anatomy lessons," *Yale Law Journal*, 113, 1519– 77, at 1544–5

Spong, Rebecca. "BTA Bank: A sigh of relief?" *Global Trade Review.* January 21, 2010. https://www.gtreview.com/news/europe/bta-bank-a-sigh-of-relief/

Sputnik International. "Agriculture is Kazakhstan's New 'Black Gold'." *Sputnik International.* October 30, 2020. https://sputniknews.com/20201030/agriculture-is-kazakhs-tans-new-black-gold-1080929222.html

Stiglitz, J.E. (Summer 2001) "Failure of the fund: Rethinking the IMF response", *Harvard International Review*, 23 (2), pp. 14-18.

Temir Bank 2009 Management Presentation

United Nations Commission on International Trade Law (UNCI-TRAL); http:// www.uncitral.org/uncitral/en/uncitral_texts/insolvency/1997Model.html;Accessed 3

August 2015

University of Windsor http://www1.uwindsor.ca/vabe/built-envi-ronment; accessed 24 August 2015

US Federal Housing Finance Agency. 'Frequently Asked Questions', http://www.fh- fa.gov/Media/PublicAffairs/Pages/Fact-Sheet-Questions-and-Answers-on-Conserva- torship.aspx), Accessed August 2014.

White & Case (23 July 2009): BTA Bank Global Steering Committee: Legal Matters Presentation

WikiLeaks, "KAZAKHSTAN: PRIME MINISTER BRIEFS BOEHNER CODEL ON ECONOMIC AND ENERGY ISSUES." 2009 August 10, 13:58 (Monday) https://wikileaks.org/plusd/cables/09ASTANA1365_a.htmlT

World Bank, World Development Indicators. http://data.worldbank.org/indicator, Accessed 1 August, 2014.

World Economic Forum (2009), The Financial Development Report (Geneva and New York: World Economic Forum, 2009), p. xi.

About the Author

Marcia-Elizabeth C. Favale wrote this book to highlight the impact a woman had during the financial crisis to then inspire other women to come forward and tell their stories. Our girls, boys, men, and women need more examples.